SEALS

SEALS

BY ALICE FIELDS
Illustrated by David Astin

An Easy-Read Fact Book
FRANKLIN WATTS
New York/London/Toronto/Sydney/1980

Thanks are due to the following for kind permission
to reproduce photographs:
Bryan and Cherry Alexander; Biofotos; Radio Times;
Hulton Picture Library

Library of Congress Cataloging in Publication Data

Fields, Alice.
    Seals.

    (An Easy-read fact book)
    Includes index.
    SUMMARY: Introduces members of the seal
family and discusses their habits, characteristics,
and commercial value.
        1. Pinnipedia—Juvenile literature. [1. Seals
(Animals)   2. Seal lions.   3. Walruses]   I. Astin,
David.   II. Title.
QL737.P6F53   599'.745   79-25260
    ISBN 0-531-03242-6

R.L. 2.9 Spache Revised Formula

elephant seal

walrus

California sea lion

spotted seal

Seals spend most of their lives in the sea.

They belong to a special group of animals called **Pinnipedia**. **Seals**, **sea lions**, and **walruses** are all Pinnipedia. The word Pinnipedia means fin-footed.

Pinnipedia were once land animals. Then, millions of years ago, they went to live in the sea. Their four legs slowly changed. They became fin-like **flippers**.

Flippers move the animals quickly and smoothly through water.

All Pinnipedia are **mammals**. (Cats, dogs, and people are also mammals.)

Like other mammals, female seals give birth to live babies. While they are very young, the baby seals drink their mothers' milk.

And like other mammals, seals breathe air through lungs, are warm-blooded, and have hair on their bodies.

Gray seal nursing her baby

6

Seals are well adapted for living in the sea.

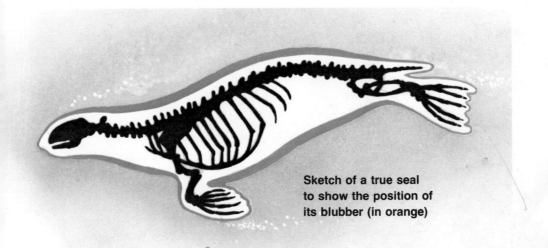

Sketch of a true seal
to show the position of
its blubber (in orange)

They have a smooth, rounded head and a long trunk that ends in a small tail. Their bodies can slide easily through water.

Underneath a fur coat, they have a layer of **blubber**. Blubber is a special kind of fat that keeps the seals warm in cold water.

**California sea lions
hunting for food**

Seals are **carnivores**, or meat-eaters. They hunt for their food in the sea.

They eat fish, squid, penguins, octopus, and other sea animals.

Seals can swim very fast, and they are wonderful divers. They can stay underwater for up to 40 minutes without surfacing to take a breath. But usually they come up for air every five or ten minutes.

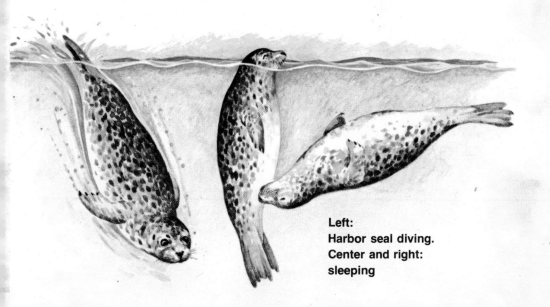

**Left:
Harbor seal diving.
Center and right:
sleeping**

While they sleep in the water, seals may float on their backs. Or, they may float with their body straight up and down. Then only the head or nose shows above the water.

Seals can also sleep underwater and come up for air without even waking up.

Seals spend a lot of time in the water. They can also live on land for long periods. On land, they usually live together in large groups called **colonies**.

Male seals are known as **bulls**. The females are called **cows**, and babies are called **pups**.

Most seals mate once a year. A year later, the cow comes ashore and has one or sometimes two pups. The pups are fed on their mother's milk. After several weeks the colony returns to sea.

Later on they come ashore again. This time they come for a short time to rest and to **molt**. When seals molt they shed their old hair and grow a new coat.

Colony of northern elephant seals

An Eskimo seal hunter

People have hunted seals for thousands of years.

Many seal hunters were people who lived by the sea. Eskimos, for example, depended upon seals. They got most of their food, clothing, and tools from parts of the seal. Nothing was wasted. Every part of the seal was used for something.

Yet these people were careful not to kill too many seals. They killed only as many as they really needed.

Some people still depend on seals for a living.

During the past 250 years, more and more seals have been killed for their valuable fur and blubber.

Seal skin is used to make expensive fur coats and other clothes. Blubber is melted down to make oil.

Today some kinds of seals are becoming **extinct** (dying out). They have been hunted so much that not many are left. A few kinds are no longer seen at all.

Articles of clothing made of seal fur

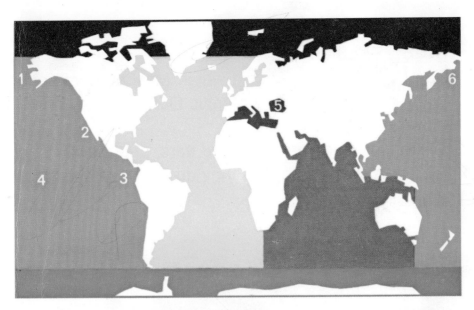

MAP SHOWING WHERE SEALS LIVE TODAY

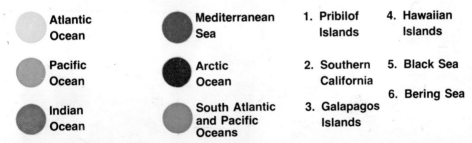

Atlantic Ocean

Pacific Ocean

Indian Ocean

Mediterranean Sea

Arctic Ocean

South Atlantic and Pacific Oceans

1. Pribilof Islands

2. Southern California

3. Galapagos Islands

4. Hawaiian Islands

5. Black Sea

6. Bering Sea

There are 32 different kinds of pinnipeds alive today. They live in many different parts of the world.

They are divided into three main groups or families. The **"true" seals** make up one group. In a second group, the **"eared seals,"** are **sea lions** and **fur seals**. **Walruses** make up the third family of pinnipeds.

TRUE SEALS

True seals live in very cold water. Most of them are found in the Arctic and Antarctic Oceans. They are known as **earless seals**.

In fact, true seals do have ears, and their hearing is very acute. But they do not have outside earflaps.

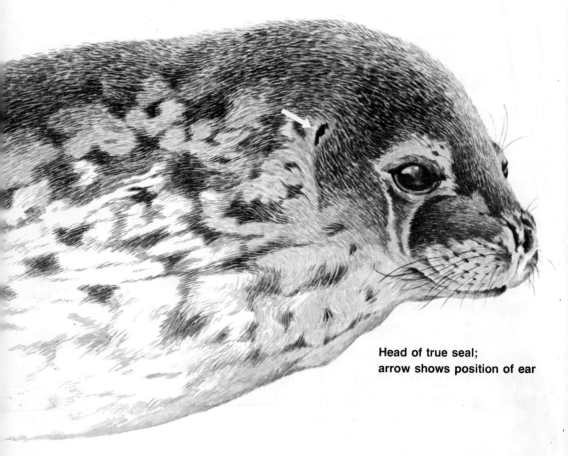

Head of true seal; arrow shows position of ear

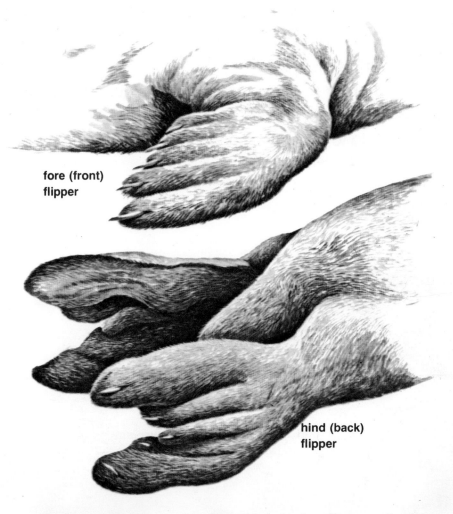

fore (front) flipper

hind (back) flipper

True seals have coarse thick hair all over their bodies.

They usually have claws on their short **fore** (front) flippers.

The **hind** (back) flippers point straight back and cannot bend forward.

Some true seals spend even more time in the sea than other pinnipeds.

In order to swim, they use their back flippers. They move the flippers and the tail end of their body from side to side. The small front flippers are used to change direction.

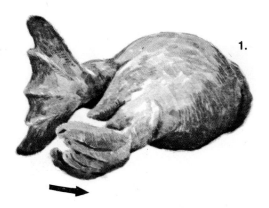

1.

View of a true seal's back flippers showing swimming movement

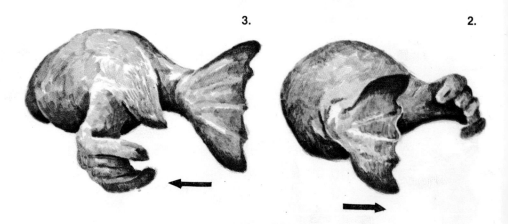

3.

2.

Gray seals, showing the
tracks they leave in the sand as
they move along on their stomachs

True seals are very graceful in the water, but not on
land.

They cannot raise their bodies and "walk." They
move along on their stomachs by wriggling like
caterpillars and by sliding.

On smooth ice they can slide along quite well.

Harp or **Greenland seals** are true seals. The adults have gray and black coats. They are about 6 feet (1.8 m) long and weigh about 400 pounds (180 kg).

Harp seals swim in very cold north Atlantic waters. They spend the summer feeding in the far north.

Adult harp seals

female

male

In the autumn, the harp seals begin to travel south. In February and March, the females crawl out onto the ice. There, they give birth to their snow white pups.

The pups molt when they are about three weeks old. The new coat is gray.

After they molt, the pups are called **graylings**.

grayling

pup

female

When the pups no longer feed on their mothers' milk, the cows and bulls mate again. From this mating will come next year's pups.

The adults stay on the ice to molt. Then they all begin their long swim back to the North.

Molting harp seals

Each year thousands of harp seals are killed by seal hunters. The hunters come in March soon after the pups are born.

Harp seal pup. Many people (called conservationists) want to stop the cruel killing of seals such as this one.

They kill the young seals by hitting them with clubs. The soft white coats of the young pups are especially valuable.

Ringed seals are among the smallest of all seals.

The bulls are about 5 feet (1.5 m) long and weigh about 200 pounds (90 kg). These seals usually live in water near the shore.

When the cows are ready to give birth, they make **caves** in the snow. Inside these **ice-dens**, the new pups are well protected from the cold. They stay with their mothers for about 12 weeks.

Ringed seals in ice-den

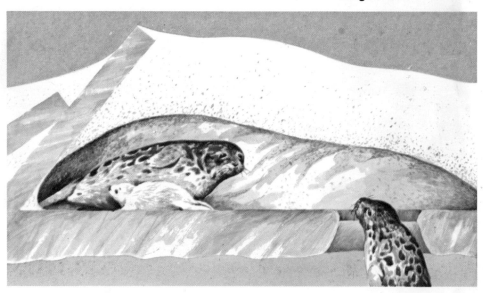

Most ringed seals live within the **Arctic Circle** or in the **North Atlantic**. Some even live in **freshwater lakes** such as Lake Baikal, in Russia.

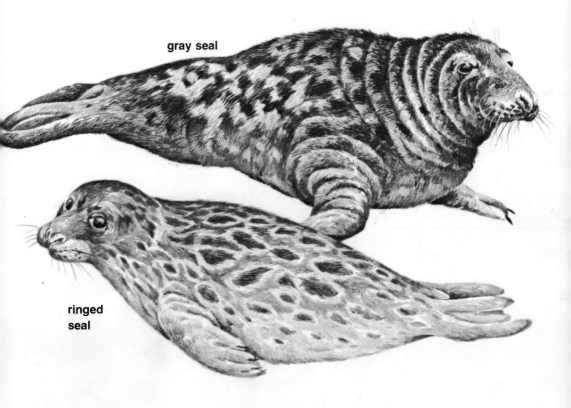

gray seal

ringed
seal

Gray seals are another species of true seals.
Although they are called "gray" seals, their spotted coats are sometimes tan or brown.

Most gray seals live along the North Atlantic coast off Labrador, Britain, and France. They are also found in the Arctic Ocean off the northwest coast of Russia.

Gray seals eat fish that people also catch for food. Some people think that too many gray seals will get the best fish before the fishermen can. So, to control their numbers, some gray seals are killed each year.

This is called seal culling.

Seal culling in the 1800s

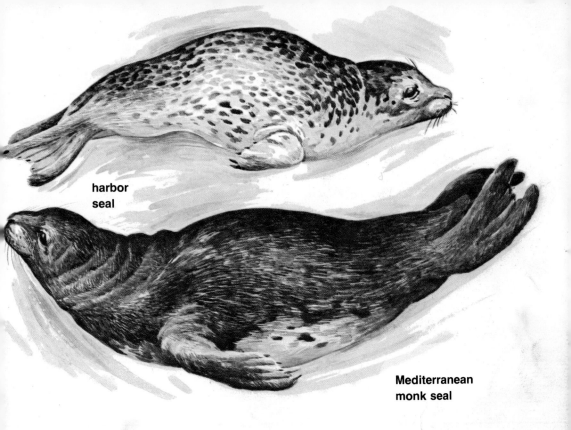

harbor
seal

Mediterranean
monk seal

Harbor or **common seals** look a little like gray seals, only they do not have long snouts like gray seals.

Harbor seals live in the northern parts of the Atlantic and Pacific oceans.

Monk seals are the only true seals that live in the warmer parts of the world.

They live in the Mediterranean Sea and the Black Sea. They are found off the coasts of North Africa. And they are seen near the Hawaiian Islands.

But monk seals are now very rare.

The **crabeater seal** is the most common seal that lives in Antarctic waters.

For a true seal, it can move quite fast on land. It can slide and wriggle over the ice at a speed of about 15 miles an hour (24 kph).

This seal has a silver-gray coat most of the year. But in the summer, the coat turns white. In fact, the crabeater is sometimes called the **white seal**.

Unlike other seals, the crabeater eats only **krill**. Krill are small shrimp-like animals that live near the surface of the water.

The **leopard seal** also lives in the Antarctic. It gets its name from the color of its coat.

The leopard seal, a fierce hunter, was once called the sea-leopard. It usually lives alone and joins other seals only during the mating season.

Leopard seals

Leopard seals will eat almost anything. Unlike other seals, they like to eat warm-blooded animals.

Leopard seals often feed on penguins and other seabirds. Sometimes they eat the pups of other species of seals.

Males grow up to 11 feet (3.5 m) long. Females are usually a little longer than males.

Fully grown leopard seals weigh from 660 to 900 pounds (300 to 400 kg).

Leopard seal chasing penguins

The **elephant seal**, or **sea elephant**, is the largest of all the pinnipeds.

The males grow up to 21 feet (6.5 m) long. They can weigh as much as 4 tons.

Head of male elephant seal

These huge animals can move quickly on land if they have to. But they prefer to lie still and sun themselves.

Bull elephant seals have a long trunk-like nose. In one species, the nose can be blown up like a balloon.

When the seal roars through this "balloon" the noise is terrific.

During the mating season, the bulls fight each other for the females. Each bull gathers a **harem** or group of cows, as mates.

Bull elephant seals fighting

Elephant seals molt early in the summer. Their hair and skin come off in big strips.

Molting elephant seals like to roll in the mud

The seals itch and rub themselves in the sand. Molting can take as long as 40 days. During this time, the seals do not eat.

When molting is over, they go back to the sea to feed. In the sea, they usually live on their own and not in groups.

There are two kinds of elephant seals. The **northern elephant seal** lives off the coasts of Mexico and Southern California.

Northern elephant seals, with pup

This seal is now protected and it is against the law to hunt it.

The **southern elephant seal** lives near islands off the coast of Antarctica. It also lives off the coasts of lower South America.

Southern elephant seals, male is in the front

Seal hunters are allowed to kill only a certain number of bulls each year.

FUR SEALS AND SEA LIONS

This group is also known as **eared seals**. They have pointed ear flaps that you can easily see.

Fur seals and sea lions can bend their back flippers forward. And their paddle-shaped front flippers are wide and strong. This means they can waddle along on land on all four flippers. They do not have to drag themselves on their stomachs.

True seals use their back flippers to swim. But eared seals use their front flippers like paddles to move through the water.

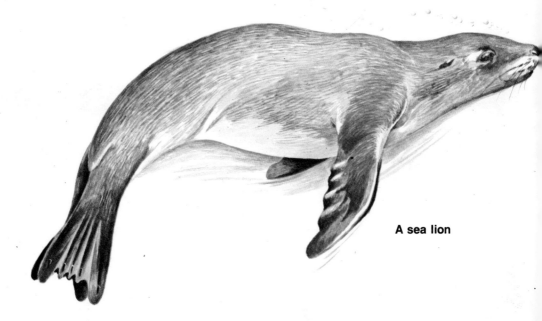

A sea lion

When they swim, their back flippers are held with the soles together. Like a **rudder**, they help to steer the seal.

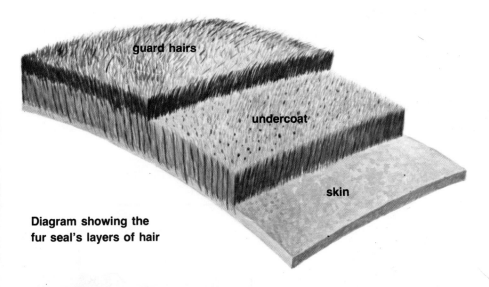

Diagram showing the fur seal's layers of hair

The fur seal has a different coat from all other seals. In fact, it has two coats.

The outside coat is made up of long stiff hairs called **guard hairs**. Underneath grows a soft thick coat of very fine hair.

This beautiful fur can be made into expensive clothing. That is why fur seals have been killed in large numbers.

The **Northern Alaskan** or **Pribilof fur seal** lives mainly in the Bering Sea. In the Pribilof Islands near Alaska they live in large groups of up to 1,500,000 animals.

These seals are known for their long **migrations**. Every year they swim thousands of miles. They mate in the spring, and in the autumn they start south.

The cows often travel 3,000 miles (4,800 km). They go as far south as California and Japan.

Alaskan (Northern) fur seals

A California sea lion performing

California sea lions do not have two coats of fur. But, like fur seals, they can bend their back flippers to walk on land.

They are very playful. You often see California sea lions performing in zoos and circuses. They are quick at learning all kinds of catching and balancing tricks.

California sea lions are found off the coast of California. They also live on the Galápagos Islands, and a few are found off the coast of Japan.

WALRUSES

There are only two kinds of walruses. They are the **Pacific walrus** and the **Atlantic walrus**. Both live mainly within the Arctic Circle. They look and act very much alike.

Like the true seals, walruses do not have outside earflaps.

Walrus resting on the ice

Walrus swimming

But like fur seals and sea lions, walruses can bend their back flippers and "walk" on land. They look clumsy, but they can move very quickly.

Walruses use both back flippers and front flippers in order to swim.

MH Country School

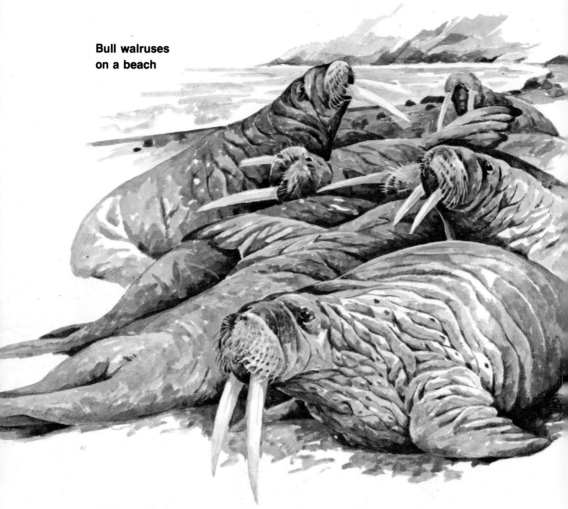

Bull walruses on a beach

After elephant seals, walruses are the largest pinnipeds.

The Pacific walrus grows up to 13 feet (4 m) long. It can weigh around 3,000 pounds (about 1,300 kg). The Atlantic walrus is a little smaller.

All walruses have rough skin with few hairs on their bodies. They do have stiff whiskers above their mouths.

The whiskers help the walrus find and guide food into its mouth.

Head of Pacific walrus

Both male and female walruses have two long tusks. These are really very long, strong upper teeth.

Young walruses, called **calves**, begin to get their tusks at four months. The tusks keep growing during the life of the animal. Tusks may grow as large as 2 to 3 feet (60 to 90 cm) long.

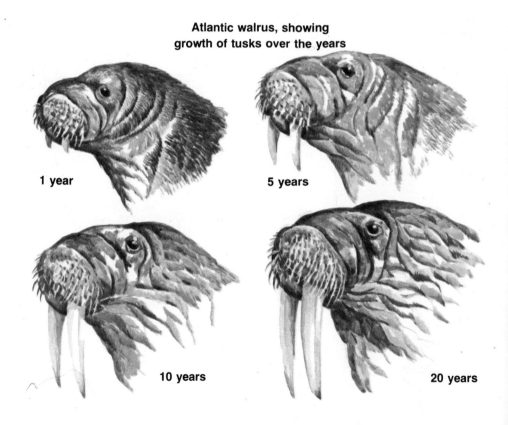

Atlantic walrus, showing growth of tusks over the years

1 year

5 years

10 years

20 years

Top: this walrus is using its tusks for support while resting on an ice floe. Right: tusks are a handy weapon against a polar bear

The walrus uses its tusks to dig for food and to fight.

Sometimes a walrus sticks its tusks in an **ice floe** and floats along getting a free ride.

The walrus family are called **Odobenidae**. It means "those that walk with their teeth."

Walruses usually hunt for food in shallow water. They stir up the sand and rocks with their tusks. Then they use their lips and whiskers to pick out the food.

They feed on clams, mussels, starfish, shrimp, and other sea animals. Walruses eat only the soft parts of an animal. They break up the shells with their teeth and spit them out.

When food is scarce, walruses will sometimes kill seals to eat. Then they are called **rogue (villain) walruses**. The rest of the walrus herd will not go near a rogue walrus.

Walrus searching for food

Walruses travel north in the spring and summer. In the fall, they travel south.

Sometimes they make part of the trip on drifting ice. During the spring trip, they also breed on the ice.

A mother walrus carries her young pup on her back

Baby walruses can swim almost as soon as they are born. Their mothers take great care of them. The walrus calves stay with their mothers for about two years. (Seals usually care for their pups for only a few months, sometimes only a few weeks.)

Walruses were once killed in great numbers. So many were killed that they were almost extinct.

The blubber was made into oil for lamps and stoves. Ivory from their tusks was used to make beautiful carvings that sold for high prices.

Today, walruses are protected by law. Only Eskimos and other native Arctic people may kill them. Even so, the Atlantic walrus is still dangerously rare.

Some ivory carvings

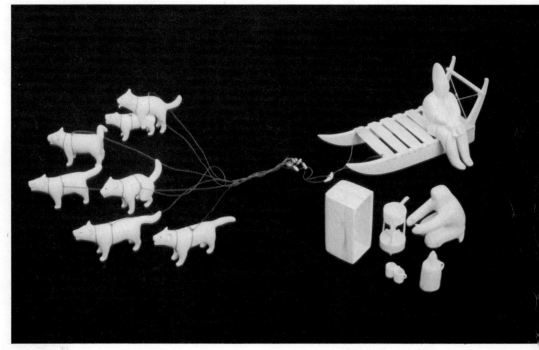

Pinnipeds have natural enemies. Seals are one of the foods that **killer whales** like. **Polar bears** hunt for their favorite food—Harbor and Harp seals. **Sharks** enjoy a dinner of seal or walrus.

But the pinnipeds' worst enemy is the human hunter. Some species may disappear forever, because we have killed so many.

Conservationists are trying to protect these animals. They have succeeded in having laws made that limit the number of seals that may be hunted.

With wise laws, perhaps we can keep from hunting the pinnipeds to the point of extinction.

INDEX